The Duty of American Women to Their Country
Condensed Edition

Catharine Esther Beecher

Contents

Bibliographic Key Phrases

American women; women's duty; female education; social dangers; religious instruction; female teachers; moral training; American democracy; school reform; national education;

Publisher's Note

Is democracy in peril? This electrifying 1845 call to action by Catharine Beecher, renowned educator and sister of Harriet Beecher Stowe, argues that the fate of our nation hinges on the education of its youth. The author uses the horrifying example of the French Reign of Terror to illustrate the dangers of an uneducated citizenry, and then she lays bare the shocking reality of America's own educational shortcomings. The document's insights into the perils of an unschooled populace, the dire situation of America's schools, and the imperative role of women in addressing this national crisis make it a must-read for anyone interested in the future of American democracy. You'll gain a powerful perspective on the ongoing struggles for public education, the importance of moral instruction, and the vital contributions women can make to building a better future.

Truth in Publishing (Disclosures)

This book, *The Duty of American Women to Their Country* (1845), is a fascinating and sometimes frightening relic of the antebellum era. It's not just a book about the importance of education—it's a cautionary tale about the dangers of ignorance, a plea to American women to act as moral guardians against the insidious spread of what Catharine Esther Beecher perceived as dangerous democratic fervor.

Now, if you're looking for a nuanced and balanced exploration of 19th-century politics, this ain't it. Beecher pulls no punches when it comes to her anxieties about the threat of "democracy gone wild." And her prose, while certainly eloquent for its time, might make some modern readers long for a good dose of Hemingway.

However, this book is surprisingly entertaining (in a morbidly fascinating kind of way). Beecher's descriptions of the Reign of Terror in France are incredibly vivid and detailed, even if a tad overdramatic. The sheer volume of detail she provides in her accounts of mob violence, prison horrors, and the guillotine is enough to make any reader's hair stand on end.

Beecher's worries about the dangers of "ignorant voters" and the perils of social unrest, while perhaps alarmist, are rooted in a real concern for the future of America. And her call to women to take up the mantle of education—to become "missionary teachers" and save the nation from itself—is both remarkable and surprisingly forward-thinking.

This book is not for the faint of heart, but for those with a taste for the dramatic, a penchant for social commentary, and a curiosity about the historical anxieties of our nation, it's a wild, albeit somewhat dated, ride.

Historical Context

Significance at the Time of Publication

Catharine Beecher's *The Duty of American Women to Their Country* (1845) was published at a time when the United States was undergoing tremendous social and political change, and was facing a number of crises. The nation was on the brink of war with Mexico. The question of slavery was threatening to tear the nation apart, and the Second Great Awakening was stirring the souls of Americans with its evangelical fervor.

Beecher, a prominent feminist and educational reformer, saw a connection between the nation's plight and the lack of proper education for its citizenry. She focused specifically on the role of women in educating the future generation and thus saving the republic. She believed that women, with their natural affinity for children, and their perceived innate moral and intellectual qualities, were uniquely qualified to educate the nation's youth, and they should dedicate their time and effort to educating the public and raising funds to support schools.

Role in Discourse in Subsequent Years

Beecher's treatise helped to shape the discourse surrounding education and women's roles in American society, and her work was often cited in the ongoing debates over the best ways to educate the nation's children. Her emphasis on the importance of women's role in education, as well as her views on the role of religion in education, were widely discussed in the years following the book's publication.

Beecher's work, with its emphasis on the need for moral instruction in schools, coincided with the rise of the common school movement in the United States. The common school movement, a key element of the Second Great Awakening, promoted the establishment of free public schools for all children, which would serve to instill in them the basic values of American society. Beecher, in her argument for the role of religion in education, helped to fuel the debate about the best way to promote moral character in schools.

Why it May Be of Interest Now

Beecher's treatise, written at a time when the United States was grappling with its own unique set of challenges, may be of renewed interest today in light of recent events and trends.

- The rise of populism and the spread of misinformation may prompt readers to reflect on Beecher's concerns about the dangers of ignorance and lack of critical thinking in a democracy.
- The renewed focus on the role of women in society, the recent #MeToo movement, and the struggle for gender equality may lead readers to explore Beecher's ideas about the importance of women's education and their ability to positively influence society.
- The ongoing debates about the role of religion in public education may cause readers to revisit Beecher's arguments about how to incorporate religious instruction in schools without offending those of diverse faiths.

Importance in Future Decades

Beecher's book may hold lasting significance for future generations, as the issues she explored — the importance of education for the success of a democracy, the role of women in society, and the debate about the role of religion in public life — will likely continue to be relevant for decades to come. Her treatise will provide future generations with insights into the challenges faced by her generation, and the role that women played in shaping the social and political landscape of the United States.

Footnotes

[1] Beecher's claims here about voter literacy and the number of criminals and felons who could vote may seem overstated to today's pro-voting-rights readers, but it's worth recalling that politics was a pretty rough business in the 19th century.

[2] Beecher's arguments about using the Bible in public schools were consistent with the views of many evangelicals in the mid-19th century. She was also influenced by the Prussian education system, which, as she notes, included the Bible as a central element of the curriculum.

[3] Beecher's views about the dangers of women working in factories are somewhat typical for the time. She was influenced by the views of many other social reformers who, like her, feared the effects of industrialization on both women and children. In this, they were not entirely wrong.

[4] The two works referred to here are *A Treatise on Domestic Economy* (1841) and *The American Housekeeper's Receipt Book* (1846).

Abstracts

TLDR (three words)

Educate women, save nation.

ELI5

This book is about why it's important for women to teach children. If children don't learn, our country will become like France during the time when the bad guys were cutting everyone's heads off! We need women to teach kids how to be good and to help them learn their letters and numbers.

Scientific-Style Abstract

This treatise argues that the United States is in peril due to widespread ignorance and a lack of moral character among the citizenry, and that only a widespread movement to educate women as teachers can avert national disaster. Drawing upon the historical example of the French Revolution's Reign of Terror, the author demonstrates the dangers of an uneducated populace and emphasizes the critical role that women play in shaping the morals and intellect of future generations. The author concludes with a plan for establishing a network of female missionary teachers to bring education to the most destitute regions of the country.

For Complete Idiots Only

If you are stupid and willfully ignorant, you may find this simple summary helpful: The United States of America is in a big mess. It has a problem with too many stupid people who won't educate their kids. That's why we need the smart women to take charge and save the country.

Learning Aids

Mnemonic (acronym)

W.O.M.E.N.

- **W**oman is a guardian and teacher of childhood.
- **O**ut of the schoolroom and into the world, women influence children as they grow up.
- **M**oral and religious principles must be taught to children.
- **E**ducate and locate female teachers! It's our best hope!
- **N**ational safety depends on these women and the role they play.

Mnemonic (speakable)

Women, Women, oh so wise!
The children need you, open your eyes.
The future depends on your guidance and skill,
So teach them with love and a heart that is filled,
With knowledge and virtue that's deep and profound,
Then America's fate will be truly sound.

Mnemonic (singable)

(Tune: "Amazing Grace")

American women, your duty is clear, Educate children, dispel all their fear. Our nation's future depends on your hand, Inspire them with knowledge, across the land.

The children are waiting, their voices are soft, They need your compassion, their hearts to uplift. So teach them the Bible, the truths that are pure, And the morals that last, that always endure.

Their hearts will be grateful, their futures so bright, With virtue and knowledge, their paths will be right. American women, their destiny's yours, To mold them with wisdom, and open their doors.

And when you are gone, and your life is complete, Their blessings will follow, your memory sweet. So answer this call, be true to your vow, Educate children, and uplift them now.

Most Important Passages

The Reign of Terror: A Warning to America

Look, then, at France during that awful period called *the Reign of Terror*. First, observe the process by which the power passed into the hands of the people. An extravagant king, a selfish aristocracy, an exacting priesthood, had absorbed all the wealth, honour, and power, until the people were ground to the dust. All offices of trust and emolument were in the hands of the privileged few, all laws made for their benefit, all monopolies held for their profit, while the common people were condemned to heavy toils, with returns not sufficient to supply the necessities of life, so that, in some districts, famine began to stalk through the land.

This passage is important because it lays out Beecher's argumentative strategy: comparing the French Revolution to the potential future of the United States. Beecher builds a powerful case by demonstrating that the French people lacked both the intelligence and the virtue necessary to properly manage a democratic government.

The Consequences of Unchecked Ignorance

Look, then, at the indications in our census. In a population of fourteen millions, we find *one million* adults who cannot read and write, and *two millions* of children without schools. In a few years, then, if these children come on to the stage with their present neglect, we shall have *three millions* of adults managing our state and national affairs, who cannot even read the Constitution they swear to support, nor a word in the Bible, or in any newspaper or book. Look at the West, where our dangers from foreign immigration are the greatest, and which, by its unparalleled increase, is soon to hold the sceptre of power. In Ohio, more than one third of the children attend no school. In Indiana and Illinois scarcely one half of the children have any schools. Missouri and Iowa send a similar, or worse report. In Virginia, *one quarter* of the white adults cannot even write their names to their applications for marriage license. In North Carolina, *more than half* the adults cannot read and write. The whole South, in addition to her hordes of ignorant slaves, returns *more than half* her white children as without schools.

Beecher's statistics, while perhaps debatable in their accuracy, reveal the core of her concern: the growing wave of illiteracy. Her argument is clear: without a commitment to education, the nation faces dire consequences. The lack of widespread literacy poses a significant threat to American democracy and its potential for success.

The Grim Reality of Poor School-houses

"The nakedness and deformity of the *great majority* of schools in this state, the comfortless and dilapidated buildings, the unhung doors, broken sashes, absent panes, stilted benches, gaping walls, yawning roofs, and muddy and mouldering floors, are faithfully portrayed; and many of the self-styled teachers, who lash and dogmatize in these miserable tenements of humanity, are shown to be low, vulgar, obscene, intemperate, and utterly incompetent to teach anything good. Thousands of the young are repelled from improvement, and contract a durable horror for books, by ignorant, injudicious, and cruel modes of instruction. When the piteous moans and tears of the little pupils supplicate for exemption from the cold drudgery, or more pungent suffering of the school, let the humane parent be careful to ascertain the true cause of grief and lamentation."

This passage, a bleak commentary from the Secretary of State, drives home Beecher's point about the sorry state of education in New York. Despite being one of the most progressive states, the conditions of its common schools are dire. The deplorable state of the schools - with their deplorable teachers - create more of a "horror" for education than a desire for learning.

The Importance of Moral Training in Education

"The universal success, also, and very beneficial results, with which the arts of drawing and designing, music, and also *moral instruction and the Bible*, have been introduced into schools, was another fact peculiarly interesting to me.

"I asked all the teachers with whom I conversed whether they did not sometimes find children incapable of learning to draw and to sing. I have had but one reply, and that was, that they found the same diversity of natural talent in regard to these as in regard to reading, writing, and other branches of education; but they had never seen a child capable of learning to read and write, who could not be taught to sing well and draw neatly; and that, too, without taking any time which would interfere with, or which would not rather promote progress in other studies.

"In regard to the necessity of moral instruction and the beneficial influence of the Bible in schools, the testimony was no less explicit and uniform. I inquired of all classes of teachers, and of men of every grade of religious faith; instructers in common schools, high schools, and schools of art; of professors in colleges, universities, and professional seminaries in cities and in the country; in places where there was a uniformity of creed, and in places where there was a diversity of creeds; I inquired of believers and unbelievers, of rationalists and enthusiasts, of Catholics and Protestants, and I never found but one reply: and that was, that to leave the moral faculty uninstructed was to leave the most important part of the human mind undeveloped, and to strip education of almost everything that makes it valuable; and that the Bible is the best book to put into the hands of children, to interest, to exercise, and to unfold both the intellectual and moral powers. Every teacher whom I consulted repelled with indignation the idea, that moral instruction is not proper for schools, and that the Bible cannot be introduced into common schools without sectarian bias in teaching."

This passage is significant because it reveals Beecher's belief that moral instruction is crucial to education, and that the Bible is the best vehicle for teaching those values. The inclusion of moral and religious instruction is essential not only to form good citizens but to develop a sense of morality in the young.

A Call to Action: Women Must Lead the Way

It is *woman* who is to come in at this emergency, and meet the demand; woman, whom experience and testimony has shown to be the best, as well as the cheapest guardian and teacher of childhood, in the school as well as the nursery. Already, in those parts of our country where education is most prosperous, the larger part of the teachers of common schools are women. In Massachusetts, three out of five of all the teachers are women. In the State of New-York and in Philadelphia similar results are seen.

Women, then, are to be educated for teachers, and sent to the destitute children of this nation by hundreds and by thousands. This is the way in which *a profession* is to be created for woman–a profession as honourable and as lucrative for her as the legal, medical, and theological are for men. This is the way in which thousands of intelligent and respectable women, who toil for a pittance scarcely sufficient to sustain life, are to be relieved and elevated. This is the way, and *the only way*, in which our nation can be saved from impending perils.

Beecher's argument is clear: it is women who must lead the way in the fight against illiteracy. Women are the natural educators, both at home and in the classroom, and women are best-suited for this task. The opportunity exists to create an entirely new profession for women - a path to financial independence, respect, and honor.

The Immense Potential of the Female Teacher

In another case, known to the writer, a young lady went into such a destitute village. There was no church, and no minister of any sect. She taught the children through the week, and also instituted a

Sunday-school. In this she conducted religious worship herself. Gradually the mothers came to attend, then the fathers, until, at last, she found herself in the office both of teacher and clergyman. The last portion of her duties she resigned to a minister, who, by her instrumentality, was settled there.

This anecdote serves to demonstrate the potential impact of female teachers. Beecher highlights the power of one individual to transform a community and how women are not only able to teach but can also inspire and lead.

The Strength of the Collective

The contract with the publisher provides that the publisher shall guaranty the sales, and thus secure against losses from bad debts, for which he shall receive five *per cent.* He also shall charge twenty *per cent.* for commissions paid to retailers, and also the expenses for printing, paper, and binding, and make no other charges. The net profits thus determined shall be divided equally, the publisher taking one half, and paying the other half to the Board above mentioned.

This passage, from the concluding section of the book, emphasizes the importance of working together for a common goal. By outlining the plan to fund a movement to educate children, Beecher suggests that collective action is the only way to accomplish such a monumental task. The power of female benevolence, when harnessed and directed, is capable of making a significant difference.

Condensed Matter

The Duty of American Women to Their Country

My countrywomen, you often hear it said that *intelligence and virtue* are indispensable to the safety of a democratic government like ours, where *the people* hold all the power. You also hear it said that our country is in great peril from the want of this intelligence and virtue. But these words make a faint impression...

The author draws a parallel with France during *the Reign of Terror*, arguing that a people without education lack the intelligence to make wise decisions and the virtue to pursue the right course. The result is chaos.

As the French Revolution unfolded, the people were "ground to the dust" by an extravagant king, a selfish aristocracy, and an exacting priesthood. The press and orators inflamed the public mind...

After a revolution that promised relief, the French found themselves more distressed than before. They believed that their problems stemmed from the "*aristocrats*," the king, the nobles, and the clergy.

Driven by rage, the people turned on the clergy, confiscating their property and driving them to exile or death. However, the promised plenty and prosperity did not follow. The mob then turned on the nobles. They were declared traitors, their estates seized, and they were doomed to banishment or death. The people seized millions of dollars in wealth through these confiscations, but this treasure, too, vanished due to mismanagement.

The people blamed the king and his "extravagant Austrian queen," and this time, the king, the queen, the king's virtuous sister, and finally the young dauphin were all brutally murdered.

Still, misery ruled. The friends of the former government were labeled "*aristocrats*" and hunted. Two parties existed: the distressed, enraged people and the trembling minority, suffering insult, fear, robbery, and often death. Commerce ceased, and the land was gripped by famine, pestilence, despair, and rage.

The people demanded an explanation. "It is the Girondists," was the reply. "They are traitors, they have been bribed, they have joined with foreign aristocrats and kings. They interrupt all our measures, and they are the cause of all your sufferings."

The mob turned on the most intelligent and well-meaning representatives, leading them to a bloody death. Robespierre, the leader of the lowest mob of all, was now the supreme dictator, and with his ascension came *the Reign of Terror*.

The author argues that the *Reign of Terror* was a war of the common people against the classes above them, fueled by individual ambition, hate, envy, and vengeance. Confidence between man and man perished, and society became a mass of warring elements. "Few men are deliberately cruel from the mere love of cruelty. Thousands, under the influence of fear, revenge, ambition, or hate, become selfish, reckless, and cruel."

The Revolution turned into a war against religion, as atheism became the prevailing principle. "By a public act, the leaders of the people declared their determination "to dethrone the King of Heaven, as well as the monarchs of the earth." The Sabbath was abolished, the Bible burned publicly, and on the graveyards was inscribed, "Death is an eternal sleep!"

The horrors of this period are staggering:

- 1,278 nobles, 750 women of rank, 1,400 clergy, and 13,000 non-nobles perished by the guillotine.
- 2,000 were destroyed at Nantz.
- 900,000 men, 15,000 women, and 22,000 children were slaughtered in the wars of La Vendée.
- 1,000 people perished at Lyons.

These horrors are not isolated to a distant land or an ancient age. The author shows that similar events have occurred in America:

- Mob violence in Baltimore, resulting in the death of innocent citizens.
- Lynching of an innocent man in the Southwest.
- American citizens *roasted alive* in the Mississippi.
- A mob attacking a house full of women and children in New England.
- The driving of black citizens from their homes and into prisons in Cincinnati.
- Citizens arrayed in arms against each other in Philadelphia.

The author argues that slavery, foreign immigration, tariffs, and economic inequality are all ticking time bombs.

The author poses a stark question: what has saved

America from the same fate as France?

The answer is: a large body of *educated* citizens.

The author turns to the U.S. Census to illustrate a troubling trend:

- *One million* adults cannot read or write.
- *Two million* children lack schools.
- In the West, more than one third of children attend no school.
- In Indiana and Illinois, scarcely one half of the children have any schools.
- In Virginia, *one quarter* of the white adults cannot even write their names.
- In North Carolina, *more than half* the adults cannot read and write.
- The South, in addition to its hordes of ignorant slaves, returns *more than half* its white children as without schools.

"We are not even stationary," the author warns. "We are losing ground every day. Every hour the clouds are gathering blacker around us."

The author then examines the conditions of the common schools in New York, where a robust school system is in place. She argues that the situation is even worse in states that have done less.

The author paints a bleak picture of the conditions children face in common schools. The schools are often dilapidated, with broken windows, unhung doors, and rotting floors. Many are exposed to the elements and located near unhealthy swamps.

The author describes the suffering of children from want of accommodations:

- Too high desks
- Lack of proper seating
- Absence of blinds or curtains to exclude the glare of the sun
- Lack of ventilation

She argues that "confinement in some of our schoolrooms is *manslaughter*."

The author describes the conditions of heat and filth in schools:

- Cracked and broken stoves
- Green, damp wood used as fuel
- No woodhouses or privies
- Schools in many cases "as filthy as the street itself."

The author also describes the use of cruel and improper punishments:

- Standing on one foot for a long time
- "Sitting on nothing"

- Holding out the arm horizontally with a weight on it
- Tying a finger so high as to oblige the child to stand on tiptoe
- Holding the head downward
- Frightening children with threats
- Severe flogging

The author argues that the shortcomings of common schools are not owing to poverty, but to "leaden apathy" and the belief that money is better spent on barns and stables. The author criticizes the neglect of moral training in schools.

The author states that the "great problem of the age" is how to secure moral and religious instruction in schools. She notes that the diversity of sects is a challenge, but that there is common ground on which all Christians agree. The author argues that moral and religious instruction in schools can be done "without sectarianism."

The author lays out a plan for moral and religious instruction in schools:

- All children should be taught that the *Bible* contains the rules of duty given by God.
- Children should be required to repeat passages from the Bible teaching the character of God.
- Children should be required to bring texts in re-

ply to questions about Jesus Christ, God, and a future state.

The author lays out a plan for moral training in schools:

- Children should be required to reflect on texts from the Bible that teach love, forgiveness, and truth.
- Teachers should use biblical precepts to counteract bad conduct and disposition.
- The benefits of good breeding and refined taste should be discussed.

The author describes ways to engage children in benevolent acts:

- Emphasize the example of Jesus Christ.
- Approve commendable actions and behavior.
- Encourage children to practice self-denial and do good.

The author argues that women are best equipped to be teachers and that they should be educated and employed by hundreds and thousands to meet the need. She presents a plan for mobilizing women in this effort:

- Mothers should seek out children to train as teachers.
- Sisters should prepare children for missionary

teaching.

- Women just returned from school should offer instruction to children in their vicinity.
- Women should seek out and support common schools.
- Women with missionary spirits should go forth to destitute villages.
- Women with wealth should support institutions for the education and location of female teachers.
- Women should circulate books, papers, and tracts on the importance of education.
- Women should encourage fathers, sons, husbands, brothers, and friends to act on the issue.
- Women should influence clergymen to promote education.
- Women should write articles for newspapers.
- Women should make occasional visits to schools.
- Women should form Ladies' School Associations.

The author argues that the Catholic Church is far more organized in its efforts to promote education through women than the Protestant Church. She criticizes the Protestant Church for failing to provide opportunities for women to fulfill their calling as teachers.

The author then lays out a plan to raise funds for educating destitute American children through the agency of women and by supporting a gentleman to devote his time to the effort. She proposes that two books be published, *A Treatise on Domestic Economy* and the *American Housekeeper's Receipt Book*. The profits from these books will be used to support the effort.

The author proposes that committees of ladies from each denomination in our principal cities be formed to carry out the work:

- These committees should secure the support of the press and the pulpit.
- They should appeal for subscriptions from women.
- They should select suitable women to be trained as teachers.
- They should provide schools for these teachers and provide for their support.

The author concludes by appealing to the generosity and patriotism of American women to act on this urgent issue.

"American mother, wife, sister, daughter, the same earthquake is trembling under your feet! If such an awful period agitates any portion of this land, it will be those raised by wealth and station as the objects of popular envy, who must first meet the storm."

"Within a stone's throw of that smiling child with golden locks, who now absorbs a mother's thoughts, may be growing up, in the darkness of ignorance and vice, the very hand that, at some awful crisis, will grasp those locks in rage, and plant the dagger in that happy bosom."

"Awake, from the dream of thoughtless pleasure! Awake from the reveries of selfish care, and save yourselves and your country, ere it be forever too late!"

Footnotes

[1] The following is the mode of obtaining the facts stated above:

In the census, 550,000 is the number of those who have *confessed* their inability to read and write. That many have claimed to be able to read and write, who are not, is thus established. In Virginia, every man, on applying for marriage license, must sign his name or make his mark. An examination was made in *ninety-three* out of 123, the whole number of the county courts giving license, and *one quarter*, and in many cases *one third*, of the applicants could not write their names. Their wives could not be any better educated. This indicates that certainly as many as *one quarter* of the white adults in the state cannot sign their names. One quarter of 329,959, which is the adult population of Virginia, is 82,489. But the census, instead of that number, gives only 58,789 who cannot read and write, a difference of *forty per cent*. Take, then, the 550,000 who have confessed their ignorance, and add *forty per cent.* for inaccuracy, and the number is 770,000. To these, add the increase since the census was taken, and those also who, by neglect, have lost all ability to read and write, and *one million* is a very moderate calculation for adult ignorance in this nation. Of these, at least 175,000 are voters. General Harrison's majority, in 1840, was 146,000, or 24,000 *less* than the number of *voters* who cannot read and write.–(*See Mr. Mann's 4th of July Oration.*)

The census also records more children as attending school than is the truth. Thus, in Massachusetts, the state records, presented to the Legislature, are very accurate, and these make the number several thousands *less* than the census. In 1840, our population was fourteen millions. *One fourth* of these are between four and sixteen, making 3,645,388 of an age to go to school. But the census, although exaggerating the number, shows only 1,845,244 as attending schools. This, deducted from the number of those of age to go to school, leaves 1,800,144, or *nearly one half,* who do not attend school. To these, add the increase since the census, and *more than half* the children of this nation are without schools!

The census also shows 4750 in penitentiaries, and their average time of confinement is *four* years. An equal number were in jails for *crime,* and their average time of imprisonment is six months. Supposing them to live, on an average, eight years after their release, and we have 85,500 *criminals* as voters.

In 1836, Mr. Van Buren's majority was 25,000. Thus it is shown, that the majority which elects our President is far outnumbered by the *criminals* who are allowed to vote.

Note A

The writer, in the preceding part, has presented a mode of religious training adapted to schools composed of children whose parents are of different sects.

There is one modification of this mode, which the writer wishes to present to that class of parents who not only believe in the Supreme Divinity of Jesus Christ, but are in a habit of addressing their worship to Him distinctively; believing that this is the way in which we have access to God the Father, who is worshipped as dwelling in Jesus Christ. Such suppose that the Bible sanctions alike the mode of addressing Jesus Christ distinctively, and also the Father distinctively, and that we can pray in either mode with acceptance.

It is believed that parents who hold this view will find great aid in the religious training of their children by adopting this method.

In commencing instructions from the Bible, let the first lesson consist of such texts as the following:

"Jesus Christ came into the world to save sinners."

"And his name is called the *Word of God*."

"All things were made by Him, and without Him was not anything made that is made."

"In whom we have redemption through his blood, even the forgiveness of sins."

"By Him were all things created that are in heaven and that are on earth, visible and invisible, whether they be thrones, or dominions, or principalities, or powers; all things were created by Him and for Him, and He is before all things, and by Him all things consist. Every house is builded by some man, but He that built all things is God."

Having thus fixed in the child's mind that the Creator of the world is Jesus Christ, and that the terms Jesus Christ, God, Jehovah, and the Lord, are different names for the same person, then let all the Bible history in the Old Testament be read with the understanding that the being spoken of through the whole of it is Jesus Christ. If any one has doubts on this point, let him read President Edwards's work on the History of Redemption, and let him also collate all the passages in which God appeared to the ancient patriarchs and prophets, and it will be clear that there was a Jehovah who *sent*, and a Jehovah who was the *messenger*, and that this last was Jesus Christ, and the one who always appeared to the patriarchs.

The advantage of this mode of commencing religious instructions is, that it presents to the mind of a child a Being who can be clearly conceived of, and a character which is drawn out in all those tender and endearing exhibitions that a child can understand and appreciate. It thus is rendered easy for parents to obey the words of the Saviour, who, when his mistaken disciples would have driven them afar off, said, "Suffer *the little children* to come unto me."

If a child is taught, from the first, to pray to Jesus Christ, all that perplexity, doubt, and difficulty which many feel in regard to Jesus Christ and the place he is to hold in their devotions will be escaped. Then, if they feel any doubts as to whether they understand correctly about the Father, and whether they are required to worship him distinctively, these doubts will easily be removed by these words of Christ.

"He that hath seen me hath seen the Father. If ye had known me, ye should have known my Father. I am in the Father, and the Father in me. The Father dwelleth in me. Believe me, I am in the Father, and the Father in me. And whatsoever ye ask in my name, *that will I do*; that the Father may be glorified in the Son. If ye ask anything in my name, I will do it."

The writer has seen a family of four children, the

youngest four and the eldest not nine, where the mother, who pursued this course, remarked that these children seemed to be aided in overcoming faults, and strengthened in doing right, by love to the Saviour, just as true Christians are; and that if they continued their present habits of feeling and conduct, she should not know where to date the time when they became pious.

There is also a mode of practical teaching in regard to *right* and *wrong*, *sin* and *holiness*, which tends much to aid a child's right apprehension of truth.

Let the child be taught that Jesus Christ created all his creatures for the purpose of making them *good* and *happy*; that it is not possible for any one to be perfectly good and happy, unless he has such a character as Jesus Christ, and that the nearer we come to possessing such a character, the better and happier we are. Then set forth the character and example of Christ, as a *perfectly benevolent and self-denying being*, living not to gratify himself, but to do good to others. Show the child that he *has not* such a character, that he is living to please himself, and not to do good, and that this is *selfishness* and *sin*. Set before him the misery to which selfishness leads, and the consequences of it, both here and hereafter.

Teach the child that the great business of life, to us all, is, by the aid of God's Spirit, *to change our characters*, in order to become like Christ; that it is a difficult work, and one that we can never accomplish without this aid from God.

Show him that all the commands of Christ are designed to keep us from doing what will injure ourselves or injure others, and that these rules are so many and so strict, that no one ever will, in this life, *perfectly* obey them *all*.

Teach him that the *true* children of Jesus Christ are those who love him, and who *earnestly are striving* to obey *all* his commands.

Set before the child the command of Christ, "Deny thyself daily, and take up thy cross and follow me," and then teach and encourage him every day to practise some *self-denial* in *doing good*.

Teach him that the more he practises this self-denial for the good of others, the more he becomes like Jesus Christ, and that the duty will become easier and pleasanter, the more he practises it.

Inquire daily, especially at the close of the day, whether the child has practised any self-denial in doing good during the day, and express satisfaction at any success.

Teach the child to pray for help to overcome selfishness, and to give thanks for Divine aid when he has performed any act of benevolent self-denial.

If any tendency to self-righteousness and self-complacency is discovered, point out his various deficiencies, or overt sins, and teach him daily to observe and confess to God his faults.

Teach him that heaven is a world where all are perfectly free from selfishness, and that those, who are selfish, could not be happy there, and will never find admittance until they become like Jesus Christ. Teach him that this life is designed as a world of trial and discipline, to free us from selfishness, and thus prepare us for heaven.

This mode, in connexion with others suggested in the previous part, if faithfully pursued, would produce results such as seldom have been seen.

These views are presented, not to oppose the views and opinions of others, but simply to induce those who hold them to act consistently with their belief.

Note B

Of the two books referred to, the first is A TREATISE ON DOMESTIC ECONOMY, BY MISS CATHARINE E. BEECHER, which has been examined by a committee of the Massachusetts Board of Education, and deemed worthy of admission as a part of the Massachusetts School Library. The following are the titles of the chapters:

1. The Peculiar Responsibilities of American Women. 2. The Difficulties peculiar to American Women. 3. The Remedies for the preceding Difficulties. 4. On the Study of Domestic Economy in Female Schools. 5. On the Care of Health. 6. On Healthful Food. 7. On Healthful Drinks. 8. On Clothing. 9. On Cleanliness. 10. On Early Rising. 11. On Domestic Exercise. 12. On Domestic Manners. 13. On the Preservation of a Good Temper in a Housekeeper. 14. On Habits of System and Order. 15. On giving in Charity. 16. On Economy of Time and Expense. 17. On Health of Mind. 18. On the Care of Domestics. 19. On the Care of Infants. 20. On the Management of Young Children. 21. On the Care of the Sick. 22. On Accidents and Antidotes. 23. On Domestic Amusements and Social Duties.
2. On the Economical and Healthful Construction of Houses. 25. On Fires and Lights. 26. On Washing. 27. On Starching, Ironing, and Cleansing. 28. On Whitening, Cleansing, and Dyeing. 29. On the Care of Parlours. 30. On the Care of Breakfast and Dining Rooms. 31. On the Care of Chambers.
3. On the Care of the Kitchen, Cellar, and Store-room. 33. On Sewing, Cutting, and Mending. 34. On the Care of Yards and Gardens. 35. On the

Propagation of Plants. 36. On the Cultivation of Fruit. 37. Miscellaneous Directions.

The other work is called the *American Housekeeper's Receipt Book*, and the following is the Preface and Analysis of the Work.

Preface (for the American Housekeeper's Receipt Book.)

The following objects are aimed at in this work:

First, to furnish an *original* collection of receipts, which shall embrace a great variety of simple and well-cooked dishes, designed for every-day comfort and enjoyment.

Second, to include in the collection only such receipts as have been tested by superior housekeepers, and warranted to be *the best*. It is not a book made up in *any* department by copying from other books, but entirely from the experience of the best practical housekeepers.

Third, to express every receipt in language which is short, simple, and perspicuous, and yet to give all directions so minutely as that the book can be kept in the kitchen, and be used by any domestic who can read, as a guide in *every one* of her employments in the kitchen.

Fourth, to furnish such directions in regard to small dinner-parties and evening company as will enable any young housekeeper to perform her part, on such occasions, with ease, comfort, and success.

Fifth, to present a good supply of the rich and elegant dishes demanded at such entertainments, and yet to set forth so large and tempting a variety of what is safe, healthful, and good, in connexion with such warnings and suggestions as it is hoped may avail to promote a more healthful fashion in regard both to entertainments and to daily table supplies. No book of this kind will sell without an adequate supply of the rich articles which custom requires, and in furnishing them, the writer has aimed to follow the example of Providence, which scatters profusely both good and ill, and combines therewith the caution alike of experience, revelation, and conscience, "choose ye that which is good, that ye and your seed may live."

Sixth, in the work on Domestic Economy, together with this, to which it is a Supplement, the writer has attempted to secure, in a cheap and popular form, for American housekeepers, a work similar to an English work which she has examined, entitled the *Encyclopædia of Domestic Economy, by Thomas Webster and Mrs. Parkes*, containing over twelve hundred octavo pages of closely-printed matter, treating on every department of Domestic Economy; a work which will be found much more useful to English women, who have a plenty of money and well-trained servants, than to American housekeepers. It is believed that most in that work which would be of any practical use to American housekeepers, will be found in this work and the Domestic Economy.

Lastly, the writer has aimed to avoid the defects complained of by most housekeepers in regard to works of this description issued in this country, or sent from England, such as that, in some cases, the receipts are so rich as to be both expensive and unhealthful; in others, that they are so vaguely expressed as to be very imperfect guides; in others, that the processes are so elaborate and *fussing* as to make double the work that is needful; and in others, that the topics are so limited that some departments are entirely omitted, and all are incomplete.

In accomplishing these objects, the writer has received contributions of the pen, and verbal communications, from some of the most judicious and practical housekeepers, in almost every section of this country, so that the work is fairly entitled to the name it bears of the *American* Housekeeper's Receipt Book.

The following embraces most of the topics contained in this work.

Suggestions to young housekeepers in regard to and domestic arrangements.

Suggestions in regard to different modes to be p
foreign and American domestics.

On providing a proper supply of family stores, o
care and use of them, and on the furniture and a
store-closet.

On providing a proper supply of utensils to be u
with drawings to illustrate.

On the proper construction of ovens, and directi
managing them.

Directions for securing good yeast and good brea

Advice in regard to marketing, the purchase of w

Receipts for breakfast dishes, biscuits, warm ca

Receipts for puddings, cakes, pies, preserves, p
catsups, and also for cooking all the various ki
soups, and vegetables.

The above receipts are arranged so that the more
simple ones are put in one portion, and the rich

Healthful and favourite articles of food for you

Receipts for a variety of temperance drinks.

Directions for making tea, coffee, chocolate, a

Directions for cutting up meats, and for saltir
curing, and smoking.

Directions for making butter and cheese, as fur
practical and scientific manufacturer of the sa
Conn., that land of rich butter and cheese.

A guide to a selection of a regular course of f
will embrace _a successive variety_, and unite
good taste and comfortable living.

Receipts for articles for the sick, and drawing
for their comfort and relief.

Receipts for articles for evening parties and d
with drawings to show the proper manner of sett
of supplying and arranging dishes, both on thes
occasions.

An outline of arrangements for a family in mode
embracing the systematic details of work for ea
the proper mode of doing it, as furnished by an
housekeeper.

Remarks on the different nature of food and drink in relation to the laws of health.

Suggestions to the domestics of a family, designed to proper appreciation of the dignity and importance and a cheerful and faithful performance of their

Miscellaneous suggestions and receipts.

The following extract from the Preface to the Domestic Economy will exhibit the origin of these two works, and some of the objects aimed at by the writer:

"The author of this work was led to attempt it, by discovering, in her extensive travels, the deplorable sufferings of multitudes of young wives and mothers, from the combined influence of *poor health, poor domestics, and a defective domestic education.* The number of young women whose health is crushed, ere the first few years of married life are past, would seem incredible to one who has not investigated this subject, and it would be vain to attempt to depict the sorrow, discouragement, and distress experienced in most families where the wife and mother is a perpetual invalid.

"The writer became early convinced that this evil results mainly from the fact, that young girls, especially in the more wealthy classes, *are not trained for their profession.* In early life, they go through a course of school training which results in great debility of constitution, while, at the same time, their physical and domestic education is almost wholly neglected. Thus they enter on their most arduous and sacred duties so inexperienced and uninformed, and with so little muscular and nervous strength, that probably there is not *one chance in ten*, that young women of the present day, will pass through the first years of married life without such prostration of health and spirits as makes life a burden to themselves, and, it is to be feared, such as seriously interrupts the confidence and happiness of married life.

"The measure which, more than any other, would tend to remedy this evil, would be to place *domestic economy* on an equality with the other sciences in female schools. This should be done because it *can* be properly and systematically taught (not *practically*, but as a *science*), as much so as *political economy* or *moral science*, or any other branch of study; because it embraces knowledge, which will be needed, by young women at all times and in all places; because this science can never be *properly* taught until it is made a branch of *study*; and because this method will secure a dignity and importance in the estimation of young girls, which can never be accorded while they perceive their teachers and parents practically attaching more value to every other department of science than this. When young ladies are taught the construction of their own bodies, and all the causes in domestic life which tend to weaken the constitution; when they are taught rightly to appreciate and learn the most convenient and economical modes of performing all family duties, and of employing time and money; and when they perceive the true estimate accorded to these things by teachers and friends, the grand cause of this evil will be removed. Women will be trained to secure, as of first importance, a strong and healthy constitution, and all those rules of thrift and economy that will make domestic duty easy and pleasant.

"To promote this object, the writer prepared this volume as a *text-book* for female schools. It has been examined by the Massachusetts Board of Education, and been deemed worthy by them to be admitted as a part of the Massachusetts School Library.

"It has also been adopted as a text-book in some of our largest and most popular female schools, both at the East and West.

"The following, from the pen of Mr. George B. Emmerson, one of the most popular and successful teachers in our country, who has introduced this work as a text-book in his own school, will exhibit the opinion of one who has formed his judgment from experience in the use of the work:

"It may be objected that such things cannot be taught by books. Why not? Why may not the structure of the human body, and the laws of health deduced therefrom, be as well taught as the laws of natural philosophy? Why are not the application of these laws to the management of infants and young children as important to a woman as the application of the rules of arithmetic to the extraction of the cube root? Why may not the properties of the atmosphere be explained, in reference to the proper ventilation of rooms, or exercise in the open air, as properly as to the burning of steel or sodium? Why is not the human skeleton as curious and interesting as the air-pump; and the action of the brain, as the action of a steam-engine? Why may not the healthiness of different kinds of food and drink, the proper modes of cooking, and the rules in reference to the modes and times of taking them, be discussed as properly as rules of grammar, or facts in history? Are not the principles that should regulate clothing, the rules of cleanliness, the advantages of early rising and domestic exercise, as readily communicated as the principles of mineralogy, or rules of syntax? Are not the rules of Jesus Christ, applied to refine *domestic manners* and preserve a *good temper*, as important as the abstract principles of ethics, as taught by Paley, Wayland, or Jouffroy? May not the advantages of neatness, system, and order, be as well illustrated in showing how they contribute to the happiness of a family, as by showing how they add beauty to a copy-book, or a portfolio of drawings? Would not a teacher be as well employed in teaching the rules of economy, in regard to time and expenses, or in regard to dispensing charity, as in teaching double, or single entry in book-keeping? Are not the principles that should guide in constructing a house, and in warming or ventilating it properly, as important to young girls as the principles of the Athenian Commonwealth, or the rules of Roman tactics? Is it not as important that children should be taught the dangers to the mental faculties, when over-excited on the one hand, or left unoccupied on the other, as to teach them the conflicting theories of political economy, or the speculations of metaphysicians? For ourselves, we have always found children, especially girls, peculiarly ready to listen to what they saw would prepare them for future duties. The truth, that education should be *a preparation for actual, real life,* has the greatest force with children. The constantly-recurring inquiry, "What will be the use of this study?" is always satisfied by showing, that it will prepare for any duty, relation, or office which, in the natural course of things, will be likely to come.

" 'We think this book extremely well suited to be used as a text-book in schools for young ladies, and many chapters are well adapted for a reading book for children of both sexes.' "

To this the writer would add the testimony of a lady

who has used this work with several classes of young girls and young ladies. She remarked that she had never known a school-book that awakened more interest, and that some young girls would learn a lesson in this when they would study nothing else. She remarked, also, that when reciting the chapter on the construction of houses, they became greatly interested in inventing plans of their own, which gave an opportunity to the teacher to point out difficulties and defects. Had this part of domestic economy been taught in schools, our land would not be so defaced with awkward, misshapen, inconvenient, and, at the same time, needlessly expensive houses, as it now is.

The copyright interest in these two works is held by a board of gentlemen appointed for the purpose, who, after paying a moderate compensation to the author for the time and labour spent in preparing these works, will employ all the remainder paid over by the

Browsable Glossary

fusillade *n.* A rapid discharge of firearms, often with deadly effect. This term is commonly used to describe a chaotic, indiscriminate killing, but the word actually describes a more strategic, military firing tactic. In the 19th century, *fusillade* referred to the discharge of multiple cannons, as described in the text.

Girondist *n.* A member of the moderate faction of the French Revolution, who opposed the excesses of the Jacobins, but unfortunately were the victims of Robespierre's Terror. The name comes from the Garonne River in southwestern France, home of the faction's leaders. The Girondists, though relatively liberal and progressive in their politics, are a reminder that even within movements for social justice, there can be a battle between those who believe in gradual, reasoned reform and those who are eager for rapid, even violent change.

Jacobin *n.* A member of the radical faction of the French Revolution, who, during the Reign of Terror, seized power and destroyed their opponents. Their name derives from a political club in Paris, originally founded by a group of intellectuals in a building named the Jacobin convent. The Jacobins believed in radical change and revolution.

mitrillade *n.* A firing technique involving multiple cannons loaded with grapeshot, firing simultaneously. This is a form of artillery barrage common in the 19th century. This was a particularly terrifying technique, because it could effectively wipe out an entire group of people.

Nantz *n.* A city in western France on the Loire River, notorious for the brutality of the revolutionary government. The city was known for its strong royalist sympathies and experienced a number of massacres.

The Decade *n.* A 10-day week, designed to replace the traditional Christian Sabbath. The Decade was adopted during the French Revolution, as part of the government's attempt to rid itself of Christianity and all its trappings. This was a symbolic act designed to sever the nation's ties to a religious past, as well as to provide a means of standardizing time within a nation that had abandoned the old calendar system.

The effort, ultimately, was doomed to failure, as the religious culture of France could not be so easily overturned, and the old system was later reinstated.

Toulon *n.* A city in southeastern France, strategically important for its harbor. It was the site of a number of massacres during the revolution. Toulon is also remembered as the site of Napoleon Bonaparte's rise to military fame when he defended the city from the English.

Vendée *n.* A region in western France, home to many strong supporters of the monarchy, who revolted against the new Republic. This revolt was brutal and ultimately unsuccessful.

Timeline

The French people are unhappy with the King and the nobles.

The French people are inspired by news of America's successful democracy.

The French people overthrow the King and establish a new government.

The French people seize the property of the clergy, the nobles, and then the King and Queen.

The French people are more unhappy than ever.

The French people demand the cause of their misfortunes.

The French people accuse the Girondists of their troubles.

The French people overthrow the Girondists, leading to the Reign of Terror.

The French people, under the leadership of Robespierre, execute thousands of their fellow citizens.

The French people are exhausted by the violence of the Reign of Terror.

The Reign of Terror ends with the execution of Robespierre.

The people of Baltimore attack the jail and murder its occupants.

Gamblers are hanged in the Southwest without a trial.

American citizens are roasted alive on the banks of the Mississippi.

A mob attacks a house in New England containing women and children.

Blacks in Cincinnati are driven from their homes and persecuted.

A riot breaks out in Philadelphia between two groups of citizens.

South Carolina threatens to leave the Union.

The American people, though prone to hasty action, are saved from the horrors of the French Revolution by their intelligence and virtue.

The American population of fourteen million has one million adults who cannot read and write and two million children without schools.

The West is the section of America most in need of education and is the most dangerous in its potential for unrest.

The South has the largest percentage of white children without schools.

The number of American voters who cannot read and write exceeds the number of voters who elected Harrison.

The number of criminals in America who are allowed to vote exceeds the number of voters who elected Van Buren.

The New York public schools, though the best in the country, are still in a deplorable condition.

Most New York schools are poorly built and lack adequate ventilation.

Most New York schools lack proper desks and chairs.

Most New York schools lack proper sanitation.

Most New York schools are taught by unqualified and sometimes cruel teachers.

American citizens, though aware of the dangers

of widespread illiteracy, do little to improve the education of their children.

The American people fund benevolent organizations for everything except the education of American children.

Sunday schools cannot provide a suitable education for children in six days, and they cannot reach the millions of children who do not attend.

The American people are warned of the dangers that await them if they do not properly educate their children.

The American people are reminded of the need to raise an army of teachers for the two million destitute children in the country.

American women are urged to become teachers for the children of the nation.

Women are reminded that they are the natural protectors of children and that they have the power to save the country.

Women are urged to take on the responsibility of educating the children in their vicinity.

American women are urged to allocate more time to educating children than they do to personal and social activities.

American women are reminded that their efforts to educate children will not only be a benefit to the country but also to themselves.

American women are challenged to think about the future and the possibility of their own children being raised in a society plagued by ignorance and vice.

The horrors of the French Revolution are used to show the potential for violence and unrest in America if the people are not educated.

Women are urged to make an effort to improve the education of children in their communities.

A plan is proposed to raise funds and create an organization to educate women as teachers.

The author describes the need for teachers and how women can be an essential part of the solution.

The author highlights the need for a person to oversee this initiative and to work towards improving the quality of education.

The author describes how Catholic organizations employ women in positions of power and leadership in education.

The author notes that Protestant organizations do not offer the same support and encouragement to women in education.

The author highlights how Protestant women have already been successful in educating and locating teachers.

The author describes the failure of a Protestant school due to the lack of a dedicated administrator.

The author points out that Protestant women are just as capable of self-sacrifice and devotion as their Catholic counterparts.

The author proposes a plan to raise money to educate and locate female teachers.

The author proposes a Board of Managers, an Executive Committee, a Treasurer, and a Secretary.

The author proposes using the profits from the sale of her books to fund the organization.

The author suggests a plan for local committees to work in unison to promote education.

The author urges women to speak to others about the need for education.

The author urges women to petition wealthy individuals and organizations to fund education.

The author suggests that women at the East help select teachers for the West, while women at the West help locate them.

The author describes the need for teachers and the potential for women to address it in the West and the East.

The author shares anecdotes to illustrate the need for teachers in the West.

The author shares stories of the success of women in teaching and their impact on communities.

The author describes a plan to raise money for educating women as teachers and to support an administrator to oversee the organization.

The author describes the need for an organization to support and educate women as teachers and to improve the quality of education in America.

The author points out that the Protestant faith should not discourage women from working in education.

The author provides examples of how the Bible can be used in schools without violating the rights of any religious group.

The author suggests that children in schools should learn to read and recite passages from the Bible.

The author suggests that children should be taught to pray.

The author suggests that children should be taught about the nature of God and Jesus Christ.

The author provides examples of prayers that could be used in schools.

The author suggests that children in schools should learn and recite passages about Jesus Christ.

The author suggests that children in schools should be taught about the importance of truth, honesty, and kindness.

The author suggests that teachers should reprimand children by appealing to the Bible.

The author suggests that teachers should reward good behavior in their students.

The author suggests that teachers should be kind and forgiving to students who have formed bad habits.

The author suggests that teachers should teach morals and character in their students.

The author suggests that teachers should make learning the Bible more engaging for students.

The author suggests that teachers should use maps, charts, and pictures to teach Bible stories.

The author suggests that teachers should teach the Bible chronologically.

The author suggests that teachers should include the Bible in their curriculum without violating the rights of anyone who objects.

The author encourages women to work toward incorporating moral and religious training into the public schools.

The author calls on women to act immediately to improve education in America.

The author reminds women that their actions can have a profound impact on the future of their country.

The author urges women to consider the future and the potential for violence and unrest if education is neglected.

The author points out that women have the power to influence the course of history.

The author reminds women of their responsibility to educate and protect children and to ensure a better future for their nation.

The author concludes by urging women to act with the same self-sacrificing spirit as Jesus Christ to promote the well-being of their country.

About the Author

Catharine Esther Beecher (1800–1878) was a prolific American author, educator, and social reformer. She is perhaps best known for her treatise on domestic economy, *A Treatise on Domestic Economy* (1841), which was a best-seller in its time and continues to be read today. Beecher was also a pioneer in the field of women's education, and she was a strong advocate for the rights of women. As the daughter of the famed preacher Lyman Beecher and sister of the renowned abolitionist Henry Ward Beecher, she moved in prominent intellectual circles.

Beecher wrote *The Duty of American Women to Their Country* (1845) at a time when the United States was still wrestling with the legacies of its founding, including issues of slavery and political instability. She felt a profound sense of urgency about the need for public education, especially for young girls, to ensure a more stable and virtuous nation. She believed that women, with their natural nurturing instincts, could make a vital contribution to national life as educators. Her work, while undoubtedly influenced by her own experience as a woman in a patriarchal society, continues to resonate with modern readers who are grappling with similar concerns regarding public education, social change, and the role of women in society. Some might compare her to modern figures like Gloria Steinem or Michelle Obama, who also strive to champion the rights and potential of women while advocating for a better future.

Beecher's legacy as an author, educator, and social reformer is vast. She wrote numerous other books and articles on a range of topics, including education, religion, and the role of women in society. Her work helped to shape the course of American social reform and continues to inspire readers today.

www.ingramcontent.com/pod-product-compliance
Lightning Source LLC
Chambersburg PA
CBHW060048050426
42448CB00012B/3146